Brands That Sell: Effective Strategies for Creating and Strengthening Brand Identities

Copyright © 2024 Reginaldo Osnildo
All rights reserved.

PRESENTATION

THE IMPORTANCE OF BRAND IDENTITY

FUNDAMENTALS OF BRAND IDENTITY

MARKET RESEARCH FOR BRAND DEVELOPMENT

VISUAL DESIGN AND BRANDING

THE PSYCHOLOGY OF COLOR IN BRANDING

CREATING A STANDING LOGO

NAMING STRATEGIES

VOICE AND TONE BRANDING

BRAND STORYTELLING

BRAND LAUNCH STRATEGIES

BRAND MANAGEMENT AND ONLINE REPUTATION

DIGITAL BRANDING AND SOCIAL MEDIA

CUSTOMER ENGAGEMENT AND BRAND EXPERIENCE

INTERNATIONAL BRANDING

SUSTAINABILITY AND SOCIAL RESPONSIBILITY

USE OF TECHNOLOGY IN BRANDING

MEASUREMENT OF THE IMPACT OF BRAND IDENTITY

RENEWAL AND REBRANDING

COMMON CHALLENGES IN BRANDING

BRANDING TRAINING AND DEVELOPMENT

FUTURE TRENDS IN BRANDING

STRATEGIES FOR SMALL BUSINESSES AND STARTUPS

BRAND PARTNERSHIPS AND CO-BRANDING

MAINTAINING BRAND RELEVANCE

REGINALDO OSNILDO

PRESENTATION

Welcome to " **Brands That Sell: Effective Strategies for Creating and Strengthening Brand Identities** ". In this book, you will find a complete and detailed guide to building and managing a brand identity that not only attracts customers but also creates a lasting connection with them. In an increasingly competitive market, a strong brand is essential to stand out, retain customers and maximize revenue.

Throughout the chapters, I will share up-to-date and practical insights that make the lives of marketers, brand designers and business managers easier. You'll learn how to define the key elements of a brand identity, conduct market research, create an impactful visual identity, and much more. Each chapter has been carefully designed to provide applicable and effective strategies, always in accessible and direct language.

This book is more than a manual; is an indispensable tool that will help you transform your brand into a true strategic asset. At the end of each chapter, you will be invited to explore the next topic, ensuring a continuous and engaging learning journey.

So, get ready to dive into the world of branding and discover how to build a brand identity that really sells.

Yours sincerely

Reginaldo Osnildo

THE IMPORTANCE OF BRAND IDENTITY

Before you start exploring specific strategies and tactics for creating and strengthening your brand identity, it's crucial to understand why this is so important. A strong brand identity not only differentiates your company from the competition, but also creates an emotional bond with customers, increasing loyalty and, consequently, sales.

THE POWER OF THE FIRST IMPRESSION

Brand identity is the first impression you leave on your customers. A well-defined brand conveys confidence and professionalism, while a poorly developed identity can turn away potential customers. From the moment someone comes into contact with your brand, whether through a logo, a website or a post on social media, they begin to form an opinion about your business.

DIFFERENTIATION IN THE COMPETITIVE MARKET

In saturated markets, differentiation is crucial. A unique brand identity helps your product or service stand out among the competition. Successful brands like Apple and Nike not only stand out for the quality of their products, but also for their strong, recognizable brand identities that resonate with consumers on an emotional level.

CUSTOMER LOYALTY AND RETENTION

A consistent and authentic brand identity builds trust and loyalty. Customers who identify with your brand tend to be more loyal, making repeat purchases and recommending your company to others. This loyalty is not only based on the quality of the product, but on the emotional connection that your brand manages to establish.

MAXIMIZING REVENUE

When customers trust and identify with your brand, they are willing to pay a premium for your products or services. A strong brand identity allows you to position your products with a higher profit margin and sustain a premium price in the market. Strong brands are synonymous with perceived value, which justifies higher prices.

Now that you understand the critical importance of a strong brand identity, it's time to delve deeper into the elements that make up that identity. In the next chapter, we'll explore the fundamentals of brand identity, defining the key elements you need to consider to create an effective and memorable brand.

FUNDAMENTALS OF BRAND IDENTITY

In this chapter, we will explore the foundations of brand identity and the key elements that make it up. An effective brand identity is built on a solid foundation, made up of several components that, together, create a cohesive and attractive image for the public.

WHAT IS BRAND IDENTITY?

Brand identity is the combination of all the visual, auditory and emotional elements that represent your brand. It includes the brand name, logo, colors, typography, language, and even the customer experience. All of these components must work together to convey the brand's message and values consistently.

KEY ELEMENTS OF BRAND IDENTITY

Brand name

The brand name is the first and most important impression you make. It should be unique, easy to remember and reflect the brand's values and personality. An effective name helps create an emotional connection with your audience and facilitates brand recognition.

Logo

The logo is the visual symbol of your brand. It must be simple, memorable and convey the essence of the brand. A good logo is versatile and can be used in a variety of contexts, from product packaging to digital marketing materials.

Colors

Colors play a crucial role in brand perception. They evoke specific emotions and associations. For example, blue is often associated with confidence and security, while red can evoke passion and energy. Choosing the right colors is essential to creating a coherent and impactful visual identity.

Typography

Typography, or the style of fonts used, also contributes to the brand's personality. Clean, modern fonts can convey innovation and professionalism, while more elaborate fonts can evoke a sense of tradition and artisanal quality.

Voice and tone

Brand voice is how you communicate with your audience. It must be consistent across all communication channels and reflect the brand's personality. The tone can range from formal to casual, depending on the target audience and the message you want to convey.

CONSISTENCY IS THE KEY

Consistency is key to building a strong brand identity. All elements must work in harmony to create a cohesive and recognizable image. This not only strengthens brand perception but also builds trust and loyalty among customers.

With the fundamentals of brand identity out of the way, we're ready to dive into how market research can inform brand identity development. In the next chapter, you'll learn how to use market research to create a brand that resonates with your target audience.

MARKET RESEARCH FOR BRAND DEVELOPMENT

In this chapter, we'll explore how market research can inform and guide the development of your brand identity. Understanding the market and your target audience is essential to creating a brand that truly resonates and meets consumers' needs.

WHY IS MARKET RESEARCH IMPORTANT?

Market research provides valuable insights into your target audience's behavior, preferences, and needs. With this information, you can make informed decisions about the elements of your brand identity, ensuring it is relevant and appealing to your audience.

TYPES OF MARKET RESEARCH

Quantitative research

Quantitative research involves collecting numerical data through methods such as questionnaires and polls. It helps identify patterns of behavior and preferences in a large group of people. This data is essential for making evidence-based decisions.

Qualitative research

Qualitative research, on the other hand, focuses on understanding consumers' motivations and perceptions. Methods such as in-depth interviews and focus groups allow you to explore the reasons behind consumer choices, offering a more detailed and contextualized view.

HOW TO CONDUCT MARKET RESEARCH

Define your goals

Before you start research, it's crucial to clearly define what you want to discover. Your goals may include better understanding your target audience, identifying market trends, or assessing the current perception of your brand.

Choose data collection methods

Depending on your goals, you can opt for quantitative, qualitative methods, or a combination of both. Online questionnaires, telephone interviews, focus groups and analysis of existing data are some of the options available.

Analyze the data

After collecting the data, analysis is the next step. For quantitative research, this may involve using statistical software to identify patterns and trends. For qualitative research, analysis can be more interpretive, identifying key themes and insights in participant responses.

APPLYING RESEARCH INSIGHTS TO BRAND IDENTITY

Defining the target audience

With insights from research, you can more precisely define your target audience. This includes demographic, behavioral and psychographic data, which will help shape every element of your brand identity.

Refining the brand message

Insights from research can reveal which messages and values resonate most with your audience. Use this information to adjust your brand's voice, tone, and core messages, ensuring they are relevant and engaging.

Developing the visual design

Research can provide insights into your audience's aesthetic preferences, helping guide your brand's choices of colors, typography, and other visual elements.

With a solid understanding of how market research can inform brand identity development, we're ready to explore visual design and branding strategies. In the next chapter, you'll discover how to create a visual identity that truly resonates with your target audience.

VISUAL DESIGN AND BRANDING

A brand's visual identity is one of the most visible and immediate aspects that consumers notice. In this chapter, we'll explore how to create an impactful and cohesive visual identity that resonates with your target audience and strengthens your brand.

THE IMPORTANCE OF VISUAL DESIGN

Visual design is more than just aesthetics; it communicates the brand's personality, values, and promise. A well-thought-out visual design can differentiate your brand, create instant recognition, and establish an emotional connection with consumers.

ELEMENTS OF VISUAL DESIGN

Logo

The logo is the central element of your brand's visual identity. It should be simple, memorable and versatile. A good logo adapts to different sizes and contexts, maintaining its integrity and recognition.

Colors

Colors are powerful communication tools. They can evoke specific emotions and associations, influencing brand perception. Choosing a color palette that reflects your brand's personality and values is essential to creating a cohesive identity.

Typography

Typography conveys the brand's personality in a subtle but meaningful way. The fonts chosen must be legible and appropriate to the tone of the brand. A well-balanced combination of fonts can add depth and consistency to your visual design.

Imagery

The images and illustrations used in visual communication

must be consistent with the brand identity. They help tell the brand's story and create an emotional connection with the audience. Choosing a visual style that reflects the brand's personality is essential.

CREATING A COHESIVE VISUAL IDENTITY

Set brand guidelines

Creating detailed brand guidelines is crucial to ensuring visual consistency. These guidelines should include specifications on the use of the logo, color palette, typography and imagery. They serve as a manual for all communication materials, ensuring that visual identity is maintained across all channels.

Keep it simple

Simplicity is key to effective visual design. Avoid overloading your identity with too many complex elements or details. A clean, simple design is more memorable and effective in communicating the brand's essence.

Consistency is essential

Consistency in the application of visual elements across all customer touchpoints is vital. This includes marketing materials, product packaging, website, social media and anywhere else your brand is present. Consistency strengthens brand recognition and trust.

With these strategies, you'll be well-equipped to create a visual identity that strengthens your brand and resonates with your target audience. In the next chapter, we will explore the psychology of colors in branding and how colors influence brand perception and consumer behavior.

THE PSYCHOLOGY OF COLOR IN BRANDING

Colors play a crucial role in brand identity and can significantly influence consumer perception and behavior. In this chapter, we'll explore the psychology of colors in branding and how to choose the right color palette for your brand.

THE INFLUENCE OF COLORS

Colors can evoke specific emotions and associations, influencing how consumers perceive your brand. Understanding color psychology can help you choose a palette that reflects your brand's values and personality, as well as resonates with your target audience.

MEANINGS OF COLORS

Red

Red is a powerful color that evokes strong emotions such as passion, energy and urgency. It is often used in brands that want to convey dynamism and intensity. However, it should be used in moderation as it can also be associated with aggression.

Blue

Blue is associated with trust, security and tranquility. It's a popular color in sectors like technology and finance, where trust and stability are essential. Blue is also a calming color, which can help create a sense of security.

Yellow

Yellow is a vibrant and cheerful color, associated with happiness and optimism. It can attract attention and is often used to evoke feelings of warmth and positivity. However, excessive use of yellow can be tiring on the eyes.

Green

Green is often associated with nature, growth and health. It's a popular choice for brands related to wellness, sustainability, and food. Green can evoke feelings of balance and harmony.

Black

Black conveys sophistication, elegance and authority. It is often used in luxury brands to create an image of exclusivity and prestige. However, black can also be associated with seriousness and formality.

CHOOSING THE COLOR PALETTE

1. Understand your audience

Color preferences can vary depending on demographics and culture. Understanding your target audience is essential to choosing colors that resonate with them. Research cultural associations and demographic preferences to make informed choices.

2. Consider brand personality

Colors should reflect your brand's personality and values. If your brand is innovative and young, vibrant, energetic colors may be appropriate. If your brand is more traditional and trustworthy, more sober and stable colors may be better.

3. Test and adjust

Don't be afraid to test different color combinations and adjust as needed. Conduct research with your target audience to see how they respond to your chosen colors and be willing to make changes to improve brand perception.

With an understanding of color psychology, you'll be better prepared to create a color palette that strengthens your brand identity. In the next chapter, we'll explore creating a striking and memorable logo.

CREATING A STANDING LOGO

An effective logo is one of the most important components of a brand's identity. In this chapter, we'll explore how to create a logo that is memorable, distinctive, and reflects the essence of your brand.

IMPORTANCE OF THE LOGO

The logo is often the first thing people notice about a brand. It must communicate the brand's identity and values instantly. A well-designed logo can create immediate recognition and establish an emotional connection with your audience.

CHARACTERISTICS OF A STRONG LOGO

Simplicity

A simple logo is easier to recognize and remember. Avoid excessive details and keep the design clean. Simplicity also makes it easier to adapt the logo to different sizes and contexts.

Memorability

A good logo must be memorable. This means it should stand out and be easy to remember after just a brief encounter. Unique shapes, distinct colors and a clear design contribute to memorability.

Versatility

The logo should work well in a variety of sizes and applications, from business cards to billboards. It should also be effective in different colors, including black and white. Versatility ensures that the logo maintains its visual integrity in any situation.

Relevance

The logo design should be relevant to the brand's industry and target audience. It must reflect the brand's personality and values, creating an instant connection with the public.

Timelessness

An effective logo must stand the test of time. Avoid fleeting design trends that can quickly make your logo look dated. A timeless design ensures your logo stays relevant for years to come.

STEPS TO CREATE A LOGO

Research and inspiration

Before you start designing, research other logos in your industry and identify what works well and what doesn't. Seek inspiration from different sources and create a mood board with ideas and visual references.

Brainstorming

Start sketching ideas on paper. Explore different concepts and design directions without worrying about perfection. The goal is to generate as many ideas as possible before refining the options.

Refinement

Choose the most promising sketches and refine them. Add details and adjustments to improve clarity and memorability. Consider different color and typography combinations to see how each element integrates into the design.

Feedback

Show your logo choices to colleagues, friends or focus groups. Collect feedback on what works and what can be improved. External feedback can provide valuable insights you may not have considered.

Finishing

Based on the feedback, finalize the logo design. Create

versions in different sizes and colors to ensure it works well in all contexts. Make sure your logo is in a high-quality format and ready to use.

Creating a striking logo is a challenging but rewarding task. With an effective logo, you can establish a strong and recognizable brand identity. In the next chapter, we will explore naming strategies to choose effective brand names that reinforce your desired identity.

NAMING STRATEGIES

Choosing the right name for your brand is one of the most important decisions you will make. In this chapter, we'll explore naming strategies to create effective brand names that reinforce your desired identity and resonate with your audience.

THE IMPORTANCE OF THE BRAND NAME

Your brand name is the first impression customers will have of your company. It should be memorable, easy to pronounce and write, and reflect the brand's personality and values. An effective name can help differentiate your brand in the market and create an emotional connection with consumers.

TYPES OF BRAND NAMES

Descriptives

Descriptive names directly explain what the company does or offers. They are clear and informative, but may be less memorable. Examples include General Motors and American Airlines.

Suggestive

Suggestive names evoke an image or feeling associated with the brand, without directly describing the product or service. They are more creative and memorable. Examples include Netflix (mix of internet and movies) and Facebook (a digital yearbook).

Invented

Invented names are words created specifically for the brand. They are unique and easily recordable, but may require more marketing effort to establish meaning. Examples include Google and Kodak.

Acronyms

Acronyms are abbreviations of the initials of a longer name. They can be effective if the full name is too long or complicated. Examples include IBM (International Business Machines) and BMW (Bayerische Motoren Werke).

Geographic names

Geographic names refer to a specific place that may be related to the company's origin or target market. Examples include Patagonia and Amazon.

STRATEGIES FOR CHOOSING A BRAND NAME

Brainstorming

Gather a diverse team and start brainstorming possible names. Don't worry about viability at first; the goal is to generate as many ideas as possible.

Competitor analysis

Analyze competing brand names to identify trends and avoid similarities. A unique name will help your brand stand out in the market.

Availability check

Check the availability of your chosen name as an internet domain and register it if possible. Also make sure that the name is not registered as a trademark by another company.

Test with the public

Testing potential names with a group of your target audience can provide valuable insights. Choose the names that resonate most with them and are most memorable.

Meaning and connotations

Consider the meanings and connotations of the name in different cultures and languages, especially if you plan to operate internationally. Avoid names that may have negative connotations.

FINALIZING THE NAME

Once you've chosen your name, make sure you register it legally and protect your brand. Use the name consistently across all customer touchpoints to build recognition and trust.

With an effective brand name, you will be well positioned to create a strong and memorable brand identity. In the next chapter, we'll explore voice and tone branding, defining how your brand communicates to ensure consistent messaging.

VOICE AND TONE BRANDING

Your brand voice and tone are essential for creating consistent and authentic communication. In this chapter, we'll explore how to define your brand's voice and tone to ensure all your communications reflect your brand's personality and values.

THE IMPORTANCE OF BRAND VOICE

Brand voice is the distinctive personality with which your brand communicates. It must be consistent across all communication channels, from the website to social media and customer service. A well-defined brand voice helps create an emotional connection with your audience and strengthens your brand identity.

ELEMENTS OF BRAND VOICE

Personality

Brand personality should reflect the company's values and mission. For example, a brand focused on innovation might have a bold, futuristic voice, while a brand focused on sustainability might have a calm, inspirational voice.

Consistency

Consistency is crucial to building trust and recognition. The brand voice must be the same across all touchpoints, regardless of channel or audience. This includes writing style, word choice, and the overall tone of messages.

Adaptability

While the brand voice must be consistent, it also needs to be adaptable to different contexts. For example, the tone may be more formal in business communications and more casual on social media.

DEFINING BRAND VOICE

Know your audience

Understanding your target audience is essential to defining your brand voice. Consider who your customers are, what their preferences are, and how they communicate. The brand voice must resonate with them and meet their expectations.

Create a brand persona

Develop a brand persona that encapsulates your company's personality. This persona must include characteristics such as values, tone of voice, communication style and even typical phrases or expressions. The persona serves as a guide to maintain consistency.

Set the tone of voice

Tone of voice is the specific way in which brand personality is expressed. It can range from formal to casual, from serious to humorous, depending on the situation. Setting clear guidelines for tone of voice helps maintain consistency.

EXAMPLES OF BRAND VOICES

Formal and professional

Brands such as banks or financial consultancies often use a formal and professional voice to convey confidence and authority.

Friendly and casual

Brands aimed at young or lifestyle audiences, such as social networks and fashion companies, can adopt a friendly and casual voice to create a closer connection with the public.

Inspirational and motivational

Fitness or personal development brands can use an inspirational and motivational voice to encourage and engage their audience.

APPLYING BRAND VOICE

Marketing materials

Make sure all marketing materials, including ads, emails, and website content, utilize your defined brand voice. Consistency in these materials is crucial to building a strong identity.

Social media

Social media is an important channel for expressing the brand's voice. Use your brand voice in every post, comment, and interaction to maintain consistency.

Customer service

The brand voice should also be applied to customer service. Train your team to communicate in a way that reflects your brand's personality and values, whether over the phone, email, or live chat.

With a well-defined brand voice, you can ensure consistent and authentic communication across all channels. In the next chapter, we will explore brand storytelling and how to use narratives to emotionally connect with the audience and strengthen brand identity.

BRAND STORYTELLING

Brand storytelling is a powerful tool for emotionally connecting with your audience and strengthening brand identity. In this chapter, we'll explore how to use storytelling to create a lasting connection with consumers and communicate your brand's values.

THE IMPORTANCE OF STORYTELLING

Stories are a fundamental form of human communication. They are more memorable and engaging than simple facts or information. Using storytelling in your brand allows you to communicate your values, mission, and personality in a way that resonates deeply with your audience.

ELEMENTS OF A GOOD BRAND STORY

Protagonist

Every good story has a protagonist. In the brand narrative, the protagonist can be the brand itself, its founders or even its customers. The important thing is that the protagonist is someone with whom the audience can identify.

Conflict

Conflict is the element that creates tension and interest in the story. For brands, conflict can be a challenge the company has faced, a problem its products solve, or a cause the brand supports.

Journey

The journey is the path the protagonist takes to overcome the conflict. In brand storytelling, this might include the story of how the company was founded, the obstacles it overcame, and the victories it achieved. The journey must be inspiring and show the growth and evolution of the brand.

Resolution

Resolution is the end of the story, where the conflict is

resolved. For brands, this could be accomplishing a mission, launching an innovative product, or contributing to an important cause. The resolution must reinforce the brand's values and mission.

CREATING BRAND STORY

Identify your values

Start by identifying your brand's core values. These values should guide the narrative and be evident throughout the story.

Know your audience

Understand the needs, desires and challenges of your target audience. The brand story should resonate with them and speak directly to their experiences and aspirations.

Develop the narrative

Build your brand narrative around the fundamental elements: protagonist, conflict, journey and resolution. Make sure the story is authentic and true, reflecting the essence of the brand.

Use multiple channels

Tell your brand story across multiple channels, from your website to social media, marketing campaigns and printed materials. Consistency is crucial to ensure the narrative is recognized and remembered.

APPLYING STORYTELLING

Marketing campaign

Use storytelling in your marketing campaigns to create more engaging and memorable ads. Tell stories that highlight your brand's values and mission.

Social media

Social media is a great channel for storytelling. Share stories about your company's founding, the impact of your products, or inspiring customer stories.

Website and blog

Your website and blog are ideal platforms for telling your brand story in greater detail. Use these channels to share your brand journey, case studies, and success stories.

With a well-developed brand narrative, you can create a lasting emotional connection with your audience and strengthen your brand identity. In the next chapter, we'll explore brand launch strategies to maximize awareness and acceptance.

BRAND LAUNCH STRATEGIES

Launching a new brand or relaunching an existing one is a crucial moment for any company. In this chapter, we'll explore effective strategies for planning and executing a brand launch that maximizes awareness and acceptance, ensuring your brand starts off on the right foot in the market.

THE IMPORTANCE OF BRAND LAUNCHING

Launching a brand is the first big opportunity to make a lasting impression on the public. A successful launch creates anticipation, generates buzz and establishes the brand's identity in the market. It's a chance to clearly communicate who you are, what you offer and why consumers should care.

STEPS TO AN EFFECTIVE BRAND LAUNCH

STEP 1 - Strategic planning

Planning is the foundation of any successful brand launch. This involves defining clear objectives, identifying the target audience, analyzing the market and developing a detailed communications and marketing plan.

Goal setting

Set specific, measurable goals for brand launch. This could include goals for brand awareness, social media engagement, lead generation, or initial sales. Having clear objectives helps direct efforts and measure success.

Target audience identification

Know your target audience in detail. Understand their needs, desires, behaviors and where they consume information. This will help you target your communication strategies and choose the most effective channels to reach this audience.

Market analysis

Perform a market analysis to understand the competitive

landscape and identify opportunities and threats. This includes studying direct and indirect competitors, market trends and possible barriers to entry.

STEP 2 - Message development

The launch message should be clear, cohesive, and resonate with your target audience. It must communicate the brand's value proposition, the unique benefits of its products or services and the company's mission.

Value offer

Develop a value proposition that highlights what makes your brand unique and desirable. This proposal should be the central focus of all launch communications.

Launch narrative

Create an engaging narrative that tells the story of your brand and what makes it special. Use storytelling elements to emotionally connect with the audience and make the message more memorable.

Message Consistency

Ensure the launch message is consistent across all communication channels and materials. This includes your website, social media, ads, emails and any other customer touchpoint.

STEP 3 - Choosing communication channels

Select the most appropriate communication channels to reach your target audience. This can include digital marketing, social media, PR, events and strategic partnerships.

Digital marketing

Use digital marketing strategies like SEO, paid advertising, content marketing, and email marketing to generate buzz and engagement around your brand launch.

Social media

Social media is a powerful tool for brand launch. Create campaigns that encourage sharing, use targeted ads to reach your audience, and actively engage with followers to build a community around the brand.

Public relations

A well-executed PR strategy can generate media coverage and increase brand credibility. Send press releases, organize launch events, and leverage influencers and brand ambassadors to increase visibility.

STEP 4 - Creating expectations

Generating anticipation before launch is crucial to creating interest and engagement. Use teaser, pre-launch and exclusivity techniques to keep your audience looking forward to the launch.

Teaser campaigns

Create teaser campaigns that give clues about the brand without revealing everything. This could include cryptic images, short videos, or social media posts that generate curiosity.

Pre launch

Offer exclusive content like free samples, product previews, or early access to create a sense of exclusivity and reward your most engaged followers.

Influencers and partnerships

Collaborate with influencers and strategic partners who can help amplify your message and reach new audiences. Choose influencers whose audience aligns with your target audience and who can authentically promote your brand.

STEP 5 - Launch execution

On launch day, the execution must be impeccable. Ensure all channels are aligned, the team is prepared, and the customer experience is excellent.

Online launch

If the launch is digital, make sure the website is optimized and prepared for increased traffic. Hold countdowns and live events like webinars or live streams to engage your audience.

Launch events

Organize launch events, whether online or in-person, to create a memorable experience. These events may include product demonstrations, keynotes, panel discussions and networking opportunities.

Customer service

Prepare your customer service team to quickly respond to questions and resolve issues. Excellent customer service during your launch can create a lasting positive impression.

STEP 6 - Monitoring and evaluation

After launch, it is crucial to monitor performance and evaluate results. Use metrics to measure success and identify areas for improvement.

Success metrics

Define and track key metrics such as social media engagement, website traffic, leads generated and sales. Compare results against established objectives to assess launch success.

Audience feedback

Collect feedback from the public to understand what

worked well and what can be improved. Use surveys, social media comments, and satisfaction analytics to gain valuable insights.

Post-launch adjustments

Based on the data and feedback collected, make adjustments to marketing and communications strategies. Continuing to refine and improve the approach ensures the brand continues to grow and strengthen.

With these strategies, you will be well prepared to launch your brand with impact and success. In the next chapter, we'll explore how to manage your online presence and protect your brand's reputation.

BRAND MANAGEMENT AND ONLINE REPUTATION

Maintaining effective brand management and your online reputation is essential to protecting and strengthening your brand identity. In this chapter, we'll explore strategies and practices for monitoring, managing, and improving your brand's online presence, ensuring it remains consistent, trustworthy, and relevant.

THE IMPORTANCE OF ONLINE REPUTATION MANAGEMENT

In today's digital world, a brand's online reputation can be the deciding factor between success and failure. Comments, ratings and mentions on social media can influence public perception and directly impact consumer trust and loyalty.

ONLINE PRESENCE MONITORING

Monitoring Tools

Use monitoring tools to track what is being said about your brand online. Some popular tools include Google Alerts, Hootsuite, Mention, and Brandwatch. These tools help you track mentions on social networks, blogs, forums and other digital platforms.

Sentiment Analysis

Sentiment analysis allows you to understand the tone of mentions of your brand, whether positive, negative or neutral. This helps you identify trends and areas that need attention. Many monitoring tools already offer this functionality, facilitating analysis.

Direct feedback

Encourage direct customer feedback through surveys, forms, and social media interactions. Not only does this provide valuable insights, it also shows that you value your customers' opinions and are committed to improving.

CRISIS MANAGEMENT

Crisis management plan

Have a crisis management plan prepared. This includes defining a responsible team, rapid response procedures and communication strategies. Being prepared for a crisis can minimize reputational damage and help resolve the situation effectively.

Quick answer

Respond quickly to any negative feedback or crisis. Quick response shows that you take customer concerns seriously and are committed to resolving issues. A quick response can prevent the situation from getting worse.

Transparent communication

Be transparent in your communications during a crisis. Admit mistakes when necessary, explain the actions being taken to resolve the situation, and keep the public informed. Transparency helps rebuild trust.

POSITIVE REPUTATION BUILDING

Quality content

Produce and share high-quality content that is relevant and valuable to your audience. This includes blog articles, videos, infographics, and social media posts. Quality content strengthens your brand image and positions your company as an authority in the sector.

Engagement on social media

Actively interact with your followers on social media. Respond to comments, join conversations, and share user-generated content. Regular engagement shows that your brand is accessible and values the community.

Reviews and testimonials

Encourage satisfied customers to leave positive reviews and testimonials. Display these reviews on your website and social media profiles to build trust and attract new customers. Positive reviews are powerful marketing tools.

BRAND PROTECTION

Trademark registration

Ensure your brand is registered and legally protected. This includes the brand name, logo and other distinctive elements. Legal protection helps prevent unauthorized use and defend against breaches.

Misuse Monitoring

Monitor misuse of your brand online. Monitoring tools can help identify cases of plagiarism, forgery, or misuse of your brand name or logo. Taking swift action against these cases protects brand integrity.

Usage Policies

Establish clear policies regarding third-party use of the brand. This includes guidelines for partners, affiliates, and influencers. Clear policies help maintain consistency and protect brand image.

EVALUATION AND CONTINUOUS IMPROVEMENT

Performance metrics

Define and track performance metrics to evaluate the effectiveness of brand and online reputation management strategies. Some important metrics include social media engagement, number of positive reviews, sentiment analysis, and website traffic.

Regular review

Conduct regular reviews of your brand management

strategies and practices. Use the data you collect to identify areas for improvement and adjust your approaches as needed. Continuous review ensures your brand remains relevant and well-perceived.

Internal feedback

Collect internal feedback from your team on brand and reputation management practices. The team's perspective can provide valuable insights into what is working well and what can be improved.

With these brand and online reputation management strategies, you can ensure that your brand remains strong, trustworthy and respected in the digital market. In the next chapter, we will explore digital branding and how to use social media to expand your brand's reach and engage your audience.

DIGITAL BRANDING AND SOCIAL MEDIA

In an increasingly connected world, digital branding and the effective use of social media are essential to expanding your brand's reach and engaging the public. In this chapter, we'll explore strategies for strengthening your digital presence and making the most of social media platforms.

THE IMPORTANCE OF DIGITAL BRANDING

Digital branding involves applying branding principles to the online environment, creating a strong, cohesive presence that resonates with digital consumers. A well-defined digital brand can increase visibility, build trust and foster loyalty.

ELEMENTS OF DIGITAL BRANDING

Web site

Your website is the foundation of your brand's digital presence. It should be visually appealing, easy to navigate, and optimized for mobile devices. Make sure your design, messaging, and content reflect your brand identity.

SEO (search engine optimization)

Search engine optimization is crucial to ensuring your website is easily found by users. Use relevant keywords, create quality content, and follow SEO best practices to improve your rankings in search results.

Digital content

Content is the heart of digital branding. Create and share valuable, relevant, and engaging content that resonates with your target audience. This includes blog posts, videos, infographics, podcasts, and e-books.

SOCIAL MEDIA STRATEGIES

Choice of platforms

Identify which social media platforms are most relevant to

your target audience. Options include Facebook, Instagram, Twitter, LinkedIn, TikTok and Pinterest. Each platform has its own characteristics and advantages, so choose the ones that best align with your goals and audience.

Content development

Create a content calendar to plan and organize your social media posts. Content should be diverse and include a mix of formats, such as images, videos, stories, polls and live streams. Maintain consistency in brand voice and tone.

Engagement with the audience

Actively interact with your followers. Respond to comments, messages and mentions. Encourage audience participation with questions, polls, and calls to action. Regular engagement helps build a loyal and active community.

Social Media Ads

Use paid ads to increase your brand's reach and visibility. Social media platforms offer advanced targeting options that allow you to precisely reach your target audience. Try different ad formats like image, video, and carousel ads.

Collaboration with influencers

Partnerships with influencers can amplify your message and reach new audiences. Choose influencers who share your brand's values and have a relevant audience. Collaborations can include sponsored posts, product reviews, and joint campaigns.

MONITORING AND ANALYSIS

Analysis Tools

Use social media analytics tools such as Facebook Insights, Instagram Analytics, Twitter Analytics and Google Analytics to monitor the performance of your campaigns.

These tools provide data on reach, engagement, traffic, and other important metrics.

Adjusting strategies

Analyze the data collected to identify what is working well and what needs to be adjusted. Try different approaches and refine your strategies based on the results. Continuous tuning ensures your digital branding and social media initiatives remain effective.

Success metrics

Define clear success metrics to evaluate the performance of your social media strategies. This can include number of followers, engagement rate, post reach, website traffic, and conversions. Tracking these metrics helps you measure the impact and effectiveness of your actions.

BEST PRACTICES FOR DIGITAL BRANDING AND SOCIAL MEDIA

Visual consistency

Maintain visual consistency across all digital platforms. This includes the use of logo, colors, typography and image style. Visual consistency strengthens brand recognition and creates a cohesive experience for users.

Authenticity

Be authentic and transparent in your communications. Audiences value honesty and authenticity, so avoid exaggerations and empty promises. Share real stories, show behind the scenes and humanize your brand.

User Generated Content

Encourage followers to create and share content related to your brand. User-generated content (UGC) can include photos, videos, reviews, and testimonials. Reposting UGC not only broadens your reach but also builds trust and engagement.

Innovation and creativity

Don't be afraid to experiment and get creative with your social media campaigns. Use new formats, explore trends and think outside the box. Innovation can differentiate your brand and keep your audience interested.

With these strategies and best practices, you can strengthen your digital presence and maximize the impact of your social media initiatives. In the next chapter, we'll explore how to create customer experiences that reinforce brand identity and promote loyalty.

CUSTOMER ENGAGEMENT AND BRAND EXPERIENCE

Creating memorable experiences for customers is essential to reinforcing brand identity and promoting loyalty. In this chapter, we'll explore strategies for engaging customers and delivering brand experiences that not only satisfy, but delight and build customer loyalty.

THE IMPORTANCE OF BRAND EXPERIENCE

The brand experience encompasses all interactions that a customer has with your brand, from the first contact to post-sales. A positive experience can turn customers into brand advocates, while a negative experience can turn off potential customers and damage a brand's reputation.

ELEMENTS OF BRAND EXPERIENCE

Customer service

Excellent customer service is critical to a positive brand experience. This includes readiness to solve problems, friendly service and the ability to personalize interactions.

Consistency

Consistency across all customer interactions and touchpoints reinforces brand identity. This applies to communication, quality of products or services and the user experience across all channels.

Customization

Consumers value personalized experiences. Using customer data to offer personalized recommendations, promotions and communications can increase engagement and satisfaction.

STRATEGIES TO IMPROVE BRAND EXPERIENCE

Know your customer

Deeply understanding your target audience is the first step

to creating memorable experiences. Use surveys, feedback and analytical data to understand your customers' needs, desires and expectations.

Create a customer journey

Map the customer journey, from brand discovery to post-purchase. Identify key touchpoints and opportunities to surprise and delight customers. A well-defined journey helps ensure a cohesive and positive experience.

Invest in training

Train your team to provide exceptional customer service. This includes communication, problem-solving and empathy skills. A well-trained team is essential to maintain consistency and quality of service.

TOOLS TO IMPROVE CUSTOMER EXPERIENCE

CRM (Customer Relationship Management)

Use CRM systems to manage and analyze customer interactions. A good CRM allows you to personalize service, track purchase and interaction history, and identify opportunities for improvement.

Feedback Platforms

Implementing feedback platforms, such as post-purchase surveys, product reviews and NPS (Net Promoter Score) systems, allows you to collect and analyze customer opinions. Use this data to make continuous adjustments and improvements.

Marketing automation

Marketing automation tools help you personalize customer communications at scale. Automated emails, retargeting campaigns and personalized recommendations are some of the ways to maintain engagement and satisfaction.

CUSTOMER ENGAGEMENT

Loyalty programs

Create loyalty programs that reward customers for their purchases and interactions with the brand. Offer points, exclusive discounts and special benefits to encourage repeat purchases and loyalty.

Brand Communities

Develop brand communities where customers can connect, share experiences and interact with the brand. Forums, social media groups, and exclusive events are effective ways to build an engaged community.

Interactive content

Use interactive content, such as quizzes, polls and live broadcasts, to dynamically engage customers. This type of content encourages active participation and strengthens the emotional connection with the brand.

MONITORING AND EVALUATION OF BRAND EXPERIENCE

Satisfaction metrics

Track customer satisfaction metrics such as CSAT (Customer Satisfaction Score), NPS and retention rates. These metrics provide insights into the effectiveness of your brand experience strategies.

Feedback Analysis

Analyze customer feedback to identify patterns and areas for improvement. Use this information to make adjustments and continually improve the customer experience.

Benchmarking

Compare your brand experience metrics to competitors and

industry leaders. Benchmarking helps you identify where you are excelling and where there are opportunities to improve.

Creating and maintaining an exceptional brand experience requires an ongoing commitment to quality, personalization and engagement. By investing in strategies that put the customer at the center, you can strengthen your brand identity and foster lasting loyalty.

In the next chapter, we will explore international branding and how to adapt brand identity for international markets while maintaining global consistency.

INTERNATIONAL BRANDING

Expanding your brand into international markets can open up new growth opportunities, but it also presents unique challenges. In this chapter, we will explore how to adapt brand identity to different international markets, ensuring global consistency while respecting cultural nuances and local preferences.

THE IMPORTANCE OF INTERNATIONAL BRANDING

Expanding into international markets requires a branding strategy that balances global brand consistency with local adaptation. An effective approach allows your brand to resonate with consumers from different cultures, increasing acceptance and success in the new market.

CHALLENGES OF INTERNATIONAL BRANDING

Cultural differences

Each market has its own cultural norms, values and consumer behaviors. Ignoring these differences can lead to misunderstandings and market failure. It's crucial to conduct in-depth cultural research to adapt your brand appropriately.

Language barriers

Language is a fundamental part of brand communication. Translation errors or inappropriate use of language can harm brand perception. Ensuring accurate and culturally relevant translations is essential.

Local regulations

Each country has its own regulations in terms of marketing, advertising and consumer protection. Complying with these regulations is vital to avoiding legal issues and building trust with local consumers.

STRATEGIES FOR BRAND ADAPTATION

International market research

Before entering a new market, conduct detailed market research to understand the competitive environment, consumer preferences and cultural differences. This helps identify opportunities and risks.

SWOT Analysis

Carry out a SWOT analysis (Strengths, Weaknesses, Opportunities, Threats) specific to each international market. This provides a clear view of your competitive advantages and the challenges you may face.

Focus groups and interviews

Conduct focus groups and interviews with local consumers to gain insights into their expectations and perceptions. This qualitative research offers a deeper understanding of cultural nuances.

Content localization

Localization goes beyond simple translation. It involves adapting content so that it is relevant and resonates with local audiences.

Translation and transcription

Hire native translators who understand the local culture to ensure accurate translations. Transcreation, or creative rewriting, may be necessary to maintain the original tone and message while adapting to the cultural context.

Visual and design

Adapt visual and design elements to reflect local aesthetic preferences. Colors, images and symbols can have different meanings in different cultures, and it is important to use them appropriately.

Brand Consistency

Maintaining brand consistency across markets is crucial to

building a strong, recognizable identity.

Global Brand Guidelines

Develop global brand guidelines that define essential elements of brand identity such as logo, color palette, typography, and voice. These guidelines serve as a standard for all local adaptations.

Local flexibility

While consistency is important, allow flexibility for necessary local adaptations. This may include tweaks to the message, image, and even product to better meet the needs of the local market.

MEASURING INTERNATIONAL BRANDING SUCCESS

Performance indicators

Define specific key performance indicators (KPIs) for each market. This can include metrics like brand awareness, market share, social media engagement and customer satisfaction.

Consumer feedback

Collect ongoing feedback from local consumers to understand their perceptions and identify areas for improvement. Use surveys, social media analytics, and focus groups to gain valuable insights.

Comparative analysis

Compare brand performance in different markets to identify patterns and best practices. Comparative analysis helps you understand which strategies work best and can be replicated in other markets.

CHALLENGES AND SOLUTIONS

Resistance to foreign trademarks

Local consumers can be skeptical of foreign brands. To overcome this, emphasize the added value of your brand and how it adapts to local needs.

Solution: local partnerships

Form partnerships with local businesses or influencers to increase brand credibility and acceptance. These partnerships can help build trust and facilitate market entry.

Competitive Differentiation

Differentiating your brand in a competitive market can be challenging. Find a unique point of differentiation that resonates with local audiences and sets your brand apart from the competition.

Solution: innovation

Constantly innovate to offer unique products and experiences that meet the needs and desires of local consumers. Innovation can be a decisive factor in brand differentiation.

Expanding into international markets requires a careful and strategic approach to adapting brand identity while maintaining global consistency. With detailed market research, careful localization, and a well-defined branding strategy, your brand can thrive in new markets.

In the next chapter, we'll explore how to integrate sustainable practices and social responsibility into the heart of brand identity.

SUSTAINABILITY AND SOCIAL RESPONSIBILITY

In today's world, consumers expect brands to not only offer quality products and services, but also demonstrate a genuine commitment to sustainability and social responsibility. In this chapter, we'll explore how to integrate these practices into the heart of your brand identity, strengthening your reputation and creating a deeper connection with consumers.

THE IMPORTANCE OF SUSTAINABILITY AND SOCIAL RESPONSIBILITY

Sustainable practices and social responsibility are no longer just competitive differentiators; they have become essential to the long-term success of brands. Consumers are increasingly aware of the environmental and social impact of their choices and prefer brands that demonstrate a true commitment to these issues.

BENEFITS OF INTEGRATING SUSTAINABILITY AND SOCIAL RESPONSIBILITY

Brand reputation

Companies that adopt sustainable and socially responsible practices are seen more positively by consumers. This strengthens brand reputation and increases customer loyalty.

Competitive differentiation

In a saturated market, sustainability and social responsibility can differentiate your brand from the competition, attracting consumers who value these principles.

Customer engagement

Consumers who identify with the values of sustainability and social responsibility are more likely to engage with the brand, promote and defend it.

Access to new markets

Some markets and consumers demand products that meet specific sustainability standards. Adopting these practices can open doors to new markets and business opportunities.

STRATEGIES TO INTEGRATE SUSTAINABILITY INTO THE BRAND

Impact assessment

Carry out an environmental and social impact assessment of your company's operations. Identify areas where you can reduce negative impact and improve sustainability.

Life cycle analysis

Conduct a lifecycle analysis of your products to understand the environmental impact at every stage, from production to disposal. Use this information to implement sustainable improvements.

Development of sustainable products

Incorporate sustainability principles into product development. This can include using recycled materials, reducing waste and improving energy efficiency.

Eco-friendly design

Adopt eco-friendly design practices to create products that are durable, recyclable and energy efficient. Consider the entire product lifecycle when making design decisions.

Sustainable operational practices

Implement operational practices that minimize environmental impact. This may include reducing energy consumption, efficiently managing waste and using renewable energy sources.

Emissions reduction

Develop strategies to reduce carbon emissions, such as

optimizing logistics, using clean energy and improving the efficiency of production processes.

STRATEGIES TO INTEGRATE SOCIAL RESPONSIBILITY INTO THE BRAND

Community involvement

Actively participate in the communities where your company operates. This may include creating volunteer programs, partnering with local organizations, and supporting community initiatives.

Volunteer programs

Encourage employees to participate in volunteer programs. This not only benefits the community, but also strengthens employee morale and engagement.

Fair work practices

Ensure that all work practices in your company are fair and ethical. This includes safe working conditions, fair wages and respect for workers' rights.

Ethical suppliers

Choose suppliers who share your values of social responsibility and who adopt ethical work practices. Conduct regular audits to ensure compliance.

Transparency and communication

Be transparent about your company's sustainability and social responsibility initiatives. Communicate these practices clearly and authentically to your consumers.

Sustainability Reports

Publish sustainability reports that detail your goals, actions and progress. These reports demonstrate your commitment and allow consumers to track your performance.

MEASURING THE IMPACT OF SUSTAINABILITY AND SOCIAL RESPONSIBILITY INITIATIVES

Performance indicators

Define key performance indicators (KPIs) to measure the impact of your sustainability and social responsibility initiatives. These KPIs may include carbon emissions reduction, amount of waste recycled, and number of volunteer hours.

Stakeholder feedback

Collect feedback from stakeholders, including employees, consumers and partners, to assess the perception of your initiatives. Use this feedback to adjust and improve your practices.

Impact analysis

Carry out periodic analyzes to assess the environmental and social impact of your operations. Use these analyzes to identify areas for continuous improvement and to communicate results to stakeholders.

CHALLENGES AND SOLUTIONS

Initial cost

Implementing sustainable practices can have a high initial cost. However, the long-term benefits, such as reduced operational costs and increased customer loyalty, can offset this investment.

Solution: partnerships and financing

Seek partnerships and funding for sustainability initiatives. Subsidy programs, tax incentives, and collaborations with NGOs can help mitigate upfront costs.

Ineffective communication

Ineffectively communicating your sustainability initiatives can lead to misperception or "greenwashing."

Solution: transparency and authenticity

Be transparent and authentic in communicating your sustainable practices. Use concrete evidence and clear examples to demonstrate your genuine commitment.

Integrating sustainability and social responsibility into your brand identity is essential to meeting modern consumer expectations and ensuring long-term success. By adopting sustainable and socially responsible practices, you not only contribute to a better world, but also strengthen your brand's reputation and loyalty.

In the next chapter, we will explore how to use emerging technologies to strengthen brand identity and innovate your branding strategies.

USE OF TECHNOLOGY IN BRANDING

Technology plays a crucial role in building and strengthening brand identity in today's digital world. In this chapter, we will explore how emerging technologies can be used to innovate branding strategies, create personalized experiences, and effectively engage consumers.

THE IMPORTANCE OF TECHNOLOGY IN BRANDING

Technology offers powerful tools to better understand consumer behavior, personalize interactions and measure the impact of branding strategies. Integrating technology into your branding initiatives can improve the efficiency, accuracy and effectiveness of your campaigns.

EMERGING TECHNOLOGIES IN BRANDING

Artificial Intelligence (AI)

AI has the potential to transform branding by offering detailed insights into consumer behavior and enabling personalization at scale.

Data analysis

AI can process large volumes of data to identify patterns and trends in consumer behavior. This allows for more precise targeting and the creation of highly targeted marketing campaigns.

Customization

With AI, it is possible to personalize interactions with consumers in real time. For example, recommendation algorithms can suggest products based on individual purchasing history and preferences.

Augmented Reality (AR) and Virtual Reality (VR)

AR and VR offer immersive and interactive ways to engage consumers, creating memorable brand experiences.

Product experiences

AR allows consumers to visualize how products would fit into their environment before purchasing. For example, furniture companies use AR to show how a sofa would look in a customer's living room.

Brand experiences

VR can create immersive experiences that transport consumers into the brand's world. For example, a tourism brand might use VR to offer virtual tours of exotic destinations.

Blockchain

Blockchain offers transparency and security, making it particularly useful for brands that want to strengthen trust and authenticity.

Product tracking

Blockchain can be used to track the supply chain, ensuring the authenticity of products and allowing consumers to verify the origin and sustainability of the items they purchase.

Loyalty programs

Blockchain-based loyalty programs can provide greater transparency and security in rewards and benefits, creating a more trustworthy customer experience.

Chatbots and virtual assistants

Chatbots and virtual assistants improve the customer experience by offering 24/7 support and personalized interactions.

Customer service

Chatbots can answer frequently asked questions, resolve

common issues, and direct customers to the right resources, improving customer service efficiency.

Personalized engagement

Virtual assistants can provide a personalized shopping experience, recommending products, helping with choices and offering exclusive discounts.

IMPLEMENTATION OF TECHNOLOGIES IN BRANDING

Identification of needs

Start by identifying your brand's specific needs and goals that technology can help achieve. This could include improving personalization, increasing engagement, or ensuring authenticity.

Choosing the right technology

Research and select the technologies that best align with your branding goals. Consider factors such as cost, ease of implementation, and compatibility with your existing operations.

Development and testing

Develop technology solutions with the help of experts and conduct extensive testing to ensure they work as expected. Test feedback should be used to make adjustments and improvements.

Team training

Ensure your team is well trained to use new technologies. Proper training is crucial to maximizing the benefits of technology tools and ensuring successful implementation.

MEASURING THE IMPACT OF TECHNOLOGIES ON BRANDING

Engagement metrics

Track engagement metrics, such as time spent on the website, click-through rate and interactions on social media, to assess the impact of technologies on consumer engagement.

Customer satisfaction

Use customer satisfaction and feedback surveys to measure the impact of new technologies on the customer experience. This helps you identify areas for improvement and adjust strategies as needed.

ROI (return on investment)

Calculate the ROI of implemented technologies, comparing implementation costs with the benefits obtained, such as increased sales, reduced operational costs and improved customer loyalty.

CHALLENGES AND SOLUTIONS

Implementation costs

Implementing new technologies can be expensive and require significant investment.

Solution: planning and prioritization

Carefully plan implementation and prioritize technologies that deliver the greatest impact at the lowest cost. Consider starting with pilot projects to test feasibility before expanding.

Resistance to change

The introduction of new technologies may encounter resistance from employees and even customers.

Solution: education and communication

Educate your team about the benefits of new technologies

and how they will improve their daily tasks. Clearly communicate to customers how technologies will improve their brand experiences.

Integrating emerging technologies into your branding strategies can provide a significant competitive advantage by improving personalization, engagement and efficiency. By taking a strategic approach and carefully measuring results, you can strengthen your brand identity and create memorable experiences for consumers.

In the next chapter, we will explore the tools and techniques for measuring branding effectiveness and understanding the impact of your strategies on brand perception and loyalty.

MEASUREMENT OF THE IMPACT OF BRAND IDENTITY

Measuring the effectiveness of brand identity is essential to understanding its impact on consumer perception and loyalty. In this chapter, we'll explore the tools and techniques for evaluating branding effectiveness, helping you fine-tune your strategies and maximize brand performance.

THE IMPORTANCE OF BRANDING MEASUREMENT

Measuring the impact of brand identity allows you to identify what is working and what needs to be adjusted. This helps ensure your branding efforts are aligned with business goals and resonating positively with your target audience.

MAIN BRANDING METRICS

Brand recognition

Brand recognition measures consumers' ability to identify your brand among others. It is a key indicator of how well your brand is being perceived in the market.

Reconnaissance Search

Conduct surveys of your target audience to measure brand awareness. Questions like "What brand comes to mind when you think of [product category]?" can help assess spontaneous recognition.

Recall Rate

Recall rate measures consumers' ability to remember your brand after being exposed to related stimuli. Post-exposure surveys, such as after an advertising campaign, can provide this data.

Brand perception

Brand perception is how consumers see and feel your brand. This includes emotional and cognitive associations that shape brand image.

Sentiment Analysis

Use sentiment analysis tools to monitor mentions of your brand on social media, online reviews, and forums. This helps you understand how consumers perceive your brand in real time.

Brand Image Surveys

Conduct research to assess brand image. Ask consumers how they describe your brand and what characteristics they associate with it. These insights can be compared to the desired brand positioning.

Customer loyalty

Customer loyalty measures the degree of commitment and repeat purchases consumers have in relation to your brand. Loyal customers are more likely to advocate your brand and recommend it to others.

Net Promoter Score (NPS)

NPS is a popular metric for measuring customer loyalty. Ask customers: "On a scale of 0 to 10, how likely are you to recommend our brand to a friend or colleague?" Sort responses into promoters (9-10), passives (7-8), and detractors (0-6).

Retention rate

Track your customer retention rate over time. An increase in retention can indicate that your branding strategies are working well.

Market share

Market share measures the share of the total market your brand occupies compared to competitors. It is an indicator of how competitive your brand is in the market.

Sales Analysis

Compare your sales to the total market to calculate your market share. Track these metrics regularly to identify trends and evaluate the effectiveness of your branding campaigns.

TOOLS TO MEASURE BRAND IMPACT

Google Analytics

Google Analytics is a powerful tool for monitoring the performance of your website and online campaigns. It provides data on traffic, user behavior and conversions, helping you evaluate the impact of digital branding.

Key metrics

Monitor metrics like bounce rate, time on site, pages per visit, and conversion rate to understand how visitors interact with your content and engage with your brand.

Social Media Analytics Tools

Tools like Hootsuite, Sprout Social, and Buffer help you monitor and analyze the performance of your social media campaigns. They provide data on engagement, reach and follower growth.

Engagement metrics

Track metrics such as likes, shares, comments and mentions to assess audience engagement with your brand on social media.

Search Platforms

Platforms like SurveyMonkey and Typeform allow you to create and distribute surveys to collect direct consumer feedback about your brand.

Creating surveys

Create surveys that measure brand awareness, perception, and loyalty. Distribute these surveys via email, social media, and on your website to get a representative sample.

DATA ANALYSIS TECHNIQUES

Trend analysis

Track metrics over time to identify trends. This helps you understand the impact of your branding strategies and adjust your actions as necessary.

Data visualization

Use data visualization tools like Tableau or Power BI to create charts and dashboards that make it easier to analyze trends and communicate results.

Comparative analysis

Compare your metrics to competitors and industry benchmarks to assess your relative performance. This provides insights into where your brand is excelling and where there are opportunities for improvement.

Benchmarking

Use commercially available benchmarking reports or conduct your own research to compare your performance with other leading brands.

CHALLENGES IN MEASURING BRAND IMPACT

Data collect

Collecting accurate and representative data can be challenging, especially when it comes to measuring perceptions and feelings.

Solution: diversified methods

Use a combination of qualitative and quantitative methods like surveys, social media analytics, and sales data to get a comprehensive view of your brand's impact.

Data interpretation

Interpreting data correctly is crucial to making informed decisions. Data can be complex and subject to different interpretations.

Solution: analytical expertise

Invest in professionals with analytical expertise or advanced data analysis tools to ensure the insights you extract are accurate and actionable.

Measuring the impact of brand identity is essential to ensure your strategies are aligned with business objectives and resonating with your target audience. With the right tools and techniques, you can evaluate branding effectiveness, adjust your strategies, and maximize brand performance.

In the next chapter, we'll explore when and how to revitalize brand identity to stay relevant in changing markets.

RENEWAL AND REBRANDING

In today's dynamic business landscape, maintaining a brand's relevance is an ongoing challenge. Sometimes this requires a complete renovation or rebranding. In this chapter, we'll explore when and how to revitalize your brand identity to stay current and competitive in ever-changing markets.

THE IMPORTANCE OF RENEWAL AND REBRANDING

Renewal and rebranding are strategic processes that can help revitalize the brand, align with new market trends, meet consumer expectations and outperform the competition. They are essential to keeping the brand relevant and powerful.

WHEN TO CONSIDER RENEWAL OR REBRANDING

Market changes

The market and consumer behavior are constantly evolving. If your target audience's preferences and expectations have changed, it may be time to reconsider your brand identity.

Example: new trends

The emergence of new trends, such as sustainability or technology, may require a brand to adapt to remain relevant.

Stagnant brand performance

If the brand is experiencing a drop in sales, loss of market share or lack of customer engagement, a rebrand may be necessary to revitalize consumer awareness and interest.

Example: decline in sales

If your sales are consistently falling, a rebrand can help reinvigorate interest and attract new customers.

Expansion or change of focus

As the company grows or changes its strategic focus, the brand identity may need to be updated to reflect this new direction.

Example: new product line

If the company is launching a new product line that doesn't align with the current brand, a rebrand can help create a cohesive and attractive image.

Compromised reputation

Reputation issues, such as public crises or negative associations, may make rebranding necessary to rebuild trust and credibility.

Example: image crisis

If the brand has suffered an image crisis, a rebrand may be necessary to distance itself from the negative event and rebuild trust.

RENEWAL AND REBRANDING STRATEGIES

Research and diagnosis

Before beginning a rebrand, conduct comprehensive research to understand current brand perception and identify areas for improvement.

Market research

Conduct market research to gather insights into consumer perceptions and expectations. Understand the brand's strengths and weaknesses and identify opportunities for improvement.

SWOT Analysis

Conduct a SWOT (Strengths, Weaknesses, Opportunities, Threats) analysis to assess the brand's current position and guide the rebranding process.

Goal setting

Establish clear and measurable objectives for the rebranding. This could include increasing brand awareness, improving perception, increasing sales or expanding into new markets.

SMART Goals

Set SMART objectives (Specific, Measurable, Achievable, Relevant, Time-bound) to ensure that the rebranding is targeted and focused on concrete results.

Identity development

Review and, if necessary, redesign key elements of your brand identity, such as your name, logo, colors, typography, and message.

Visual rebranding

Update the brand's visual elements to reflect a modern image aligned with new objectives. This could include a new logo, color palette and packaging design.

Verbal rebranding

Review brand voice and tone to ensure communications are consistent and resonate with target audiences. Update taglines, marketing messages, and brand storytelling.

Rebranding Implementation

Plan and execute the rebranding implementation in a comprehensive and coordinated manner, ensuring that all parts of the organization are aligned.

Release plan

Develop a detailed launch plan that includes all necessary steps, from creating marketing materials to staff training. Establish a realistic timeline for implementation.

Internal communication

Ensure all employees understand and are aligned with the new brand positioning. Conduct training and information sessions to explain the changes and how they impact daily work.

Communication to the Public

Communicate the rebranding to the public clearly and effectively, explaining the reasons behind the change and the benefits for consumers.

Communication campaigns

Launch communication campaigns that promote the new brand positioning. Use multiple channels, including social media, email marketing, advertising and PR, to achieve maximum exposure.

Consumer engagement

Engage consumers in the rebranding process by encouraging feedback and interaction. This can include contests, polls, and launch events.

MEASURING REBRANDING SUCCESS

Metrics monitoring

Track the metrics defined in the rebranding objectives to assess your success. This can include increased brand recognition, improved perception, sales growth and market expansion.

Performance indicators

Use key performance indicators (KPIs) to measure the impact of the rebrand. Monitor metrics like website traffic, social media engagement, customer feedback, and sales performance.

Consumer feedback

Collect consumer feedback to understand how the rebrand was received. Use surveys, social media analytics, and focus groups to gain in-depth insights.

Satisfaction surveys

Conduct satisfaction surveys to assess consumer perception of the brand's new positioning. Identify areas of success and opportunities for improvement.

Comparative analysis

Compare brand performance before and after rebranding to assess the impact of the changes. This may include analysis of sales, market share and customer engagement.

Progress Reports

Create regular progress reports to track the impact of the rebrand over time. Use these reports to adjust strategies as needed.

CHALLENGES AND SOLUTIONS

Resistance to change

Consumers and employees may resist brand changes, especially if they have an emotional attachment to the old identity.

Solution: clear communication

Clearly communicate the reasons and benefits of rebranding. Involve consumers and employees in the process to get their support and feedback.

High costs

Rebranding can be expensive, especially if it involves significant changes to products, packaging and marketing.

Solution: financial planning

Carefully plan your rebranding budget and look for ways to optimize costs, such as reusing existing materials and rolling out phases.

Renewal and rebranding are vital processes for maintaining brand relevance in ever-changing markets. With a strategic approach focused on clear objectives, you can revitalize your brand identity, increase positive perception and drive long-term success.

In the next chapter, we'll explore common challenges in branding and how to navigate frequent obstacles in brand development and management.

COMMON CHALLENGES IN BRANDING

Developing and managing an effective brand can be a complex process, full of challenges. In this chapter, we'll explore the most frequent obstacles companies face in branding and how to overcome them to build a strong, sustainable brand identity.

IDENTIFYING AND OVERCOMING CHALLENGES

Inconsistency in brand identity

Inconsistency in brand communication and presentation can confuse consumers and dilute brand identity.

Common cause

- Lack of clear and detailed brand guidelines.
- Different teams and departments not aligned with the brand's vision and values.

Solution: Brand Guidelines

- Develop a comprehensive brand guidelines manual that includes visual (logo, colors, typography) and verbal (voice, tone, key messages) elements.
- Ensure all employees and partners are familiar with and aligned with these guidelines.
- Conduct regular training and brand identity updates to maintain consistency.

Lack of clarity in the value proposition

An unclear value proposition can make it difficult to differentiate the brand in the market and confuse consumers about what the brand really offers.

Common cause

- Scattered or contradictory marketing messages.
- Insufficient focus on unique brand benefits.

Solution: clear definition of the value proposition

- Identify the unique benefits and core values your brand offers.
- Communicate these benefits clearly and consistently across all customer touchpoints.
- Use stories and concrete examples to illustrate the brand's value proposition.

Misalignment with the target audience

Not understanding or meeting the needs and expectations of your target audience can result in ineffective branding campaigns and lost customers.

Common cause

- Inadequate or outdated market research.
- Lack of segmentation and personalization in communications.

Solution: market research and segmentation

- Conduct regular market research to better understand your target audience's behavior, needs, and preferences.
- Segment your target audience based on demographics, psychographics, and behavioral data.
- Personalize communications and offers for each segment to increase relevance and engagement.

Intense competition

In saturated markets, standing out among competitors can be a huge challenge.

Common cause

- Similar products and services on the market.
- Lack of innovation and differentiation.

Solution: innovation and differentiation

- Continuously innovate your products, services and customer experiences.
- Highlight the unique aspects of your brand that set it apart from the competition.
- Use creative and authentic campaigns to attract attention and stand out in the market.

Reputation crises

Reputation crises can seriously damage brand image and consumer trust.

Common cause

- Public errors, such as defective products or poor customer service.
- Negative reactions on social networks or in the media.

Solution: crisis management and transparent communication

- Develop a crisis management plan that includes procedures for rapid response and clear communication.
- Be transparent and honest with consumers during a crisis. Admit mistakes, explain corrective actions, and keep the public informed.
- Monitor social media and media to quickly respond to any negative feedback and control the narrative.

Maintaining brand relevance

Maintaining brand relevance over time can be challenging in an ever-changing market.

Common cause

- Lack of adaptation to new trends and changes in

consumer behavior.
- Stagnation in product innovation and marketing.

Solution: continuous adaptation and innovation

- Pay attention to market trends and consumer behavior. Adapt your branding strategies as needed.
- Invest in research and development to maintain innovation in products and services.
- Periodically refresh your brand to reflect changes in the market and consumer expectations.

TOOLS AND TECHNIQUES FOR OVERCOMING CHALLENGES

Market Research Tools

Use tools like Google Trends, SurveyMonkey and SEMrush to collect data and insights about market and consumer behavior.

Social media management platforms

Tools like Hootsuite , Sprout Social, and Buffer help monitor and manage a brand's social media presence, making it easier to quickly respond to crises and engage with consumers.

Data Analysis Software

Platforms like Google Analytics, Tableau and Power BI allow you to analyze large volumes of data to make informed decisions about branding and marketing strategies.

Navigating common branding challenges requires a strategic and adaptive approach. By identifying specific obstacles and implementing effective solutions, you can strengthen your brand identity and ensure your long-term success.

In the next chapter, we'll explore the educational resources and training available for branding professionals, helping you continue to improve your skills and knowledge.

BRANDING TRAINING AND DEVELOPMENT

Branding is a dynamic discipline that requires up-to-date knowledge and refined skills. In this chapter, we'll explore the educational resources and training available for branding professionals, helping you continue to hone your skills and stay ahead in the competitive marketplace.

THE IMPORTANCE OF TRAINING AND DEVELOPMENT

Staying up to date with the latest branding trends, techniques and tools is crucial to developing effective and innovative strategies. Continuous training allows branding professionals to improve their skills, expand their knowledge and adapt to changes in the market.

EDUCATIONAL RESOURCES IN BRANDING

Online courses

Online courses are an excellent way to acquire new knowledge and skills at your own pace. Platforms like Coursera, Udemy, and LinkedIn Learning offer a wide variety of courses focused on branding and marketing.

Coursera

- **Courses from renowned universities:** Offers branding courses taught by institutions such as the University of London and the University of Illinois.
- **Certifications:** Many courses offer recognized certificates that can be added to your resume.

Udemy

- **Practical courses:** Provides practical and specific courses on various aspects of branding, from creating a visual identity to digital marketing strategies.
- **Accessibility:** Courses are often offered at discounted prices, making them accessible to a wide audience.

LinkedIn Learning

- **LinkedIn Integration:** Allows you to showcase your new skills directly on your LinkedIn profile.
- **Variety of Topics:** Offers comprehensive courses that cover everything from the basics of branding to advanced topics like personal branding and brand management.

Graduate programs

For more in-depth training, consider graduate programs in branding and marketing. Universities around the world offer specialized MBAs and master's degrees that provide a comprehensive understanding of branding theory and practice.

Program examples

- **MBA in Marketing:** Universities such as Harvard, Wharton and Stanford offer MBA programs with a strong emphasis on branding and marketing strategies.
- **Master's degree in branding:** Institutions such as the School of Visual Arts in New York offer specific programs focused on design and brand management.

Workshops and Conferences

Workshops and conferences provide valuable opportunities to learn from industry experts, exchange experiences with other professionals and discover the latest trends and innovations.

Important conferences

- **SXSW (South by Southwest):** An annual conference that covers a wide range of topics, including branding, innovation and digital marketing.
- **Cannes Lions International Festival of Creativity:** A flagship event in the marketing and advertising

industry, where you can learn about the most creative and effective branding campaigns.
- **Brand New Conference:** Focused on brand identity, this conference brings together designers and strategists to discuss and share best practices in brand development.

Books and publications

Books written by branding experts are valuable resources to deepen your knowledge. Plus, industry magazines and blogs keep you up to date with the latest trends and case studies.

Recommended Books

- **"Building a StoryBrand" by Donald Miller:** Focuses on how to create a clear and engaging message for your brand.
- **"How Brands Grow" by Byron Sharp:** Offers research-based insights into brand growth and consumer behavior.
- **"The Brand Gap" by Marty Neumeier:** Explores how to close the gap between business strategy and brand design.

Online publications

- **Adweek:** Offers news, analysis and trends in the advertising and branding industry.
- **Branding Strategy Insider:** A blog that provides in-depth insights into branding strategies, case studies, and trends.
- **Harvard Business Review:** Publishes articles and case studies on brand management and marketing in a comprehensive manner.

PROFESSIONAL TRAININGS

Professional certifications

Specific certifications can validate your skills and increase your credibility in the branding field. Organizations such as the American Marketing Association (AMA) and the Digital Marketing Institute (DMI) offer globally recognized certifications.

AMA Professional Certified Marketer (PCM)

- **Comprehensive coverage:** Offers certifications in areas such as digital marketing, content management, and branding.
- **Industry recognition:** AMA certifications are widely recognized and valued by employers.

DMI Certified Digital Marketing Professional

- **Focus on digital:** Covers all aspects of digital marketing, including digital branding, SEO and social media.
- **Regular updates:** Courses are regularly updated to reflect the latest market trends and practices.

Mentoring and coaching

Finding a mentor or coach can significantly accelerate your professional development. Experienced mentors can provide guidance, share practical knowledge, and help you avoid common pitfalls.

Benefits of mentoring

- **Career development:** Mentors can offer career development advice, helping you achieve your professional goals.
- **Practical learning:** Mentors share real-world experiences and lessons learned that are valuable to your growth.

How to find a mentor

- **Professional networks:** Use professional networks like LinkedIn to find potential mentors in your area of interest.
- **Mentoring programs:** Participate in mentoring programs offered by professional associations and educational institutions.

BRANDING COMMUNITIES AND NETWORKS

Professional Associations

Associations like the American Marketing Association (AMA) and the Chartered Institute of Marketing (CIM) offer resources, events, and networking for marketing and branding professionals.

Membership Benefits

- **Access to resources:** Members have access to exclusive resources such as surveys, webinars and workshops.
- **Networking opportunities:** Participate in events and forums to meet other professionals in the sector and exchange experiences.

Online groups and forums

LinkedIn groups, specialized forums and online communities are great places to discuss trends, share knowledge and resolve questions related to branding.

Examples of online communities

- **LinkedIn Groups:** Join groups like "Brand Management" and "MarketingProfs" for discussions and updates on branding.
- **Reddit:** Subreddits like r/marketing and r/branding offer spaces to exchange ideas and get feedback on branding strategies.

Ongoing training and development is essential to staying competitive and effective in the field of branding. By leveraging educational resources, certifications, mentoring, and professional networks, you can enhance your skills, expand your knowledge, and advance your career.

In the next chapter, we will explore future trends in branding, anticipating changes and innovations that will shape the field in the years to come.

FUTURE TRENDS IN BRANDING

The field of branding is constantly evolving, driven by technological, behavioral and market changes. In this chapter, we'll explore the emerging trends that are shaping the future of branding and how you can anticipate and leverage these changes to keep your brand relevant and competitive.

THE EVOLUTION OF BRANDING

As the world becomes more digital and interconnected, brands must adapt to new consumer expectations and technological innovations. Future trends in branding reflect this transformation and offer opportunities to create more engaging and meaningful experiences.

EMERGING TRENDS

Mass Customization

Modern consumers expect personalized experiences that meet their individual needs and preferences. Mass customization is becoming a key strategy for creating deeper, more engaged connections with customers.

Personalization Technologies

- **Artificial Intelligence (AI):** AI algorithms can analyze large volumes of data to personalize product recommendations, marketing communications, and user experiences.
- **Machine Learning:** Machine learning allows you to adapt campaigns in real time based on consumer behavior, increasing relevance and effectiveness.

Application examples

- **Netflix:** Uses AI to personalize content recommendations based on users' viewing history and preferences.
- **Amazon:** Delivers highly personalized product recommendations, increasing conversion likelihood

and customer satisfaction.

Immersive experiences

Technologies like augmented reality (AR) and virtual reality (VR) are transforming the way brands connect with consumers, creating immersive and interactive experiences.

Augmented Reality (AR)

- **Product visualization:** AR allows consumers to visualize products in their environment before purchasing, increasing confidence in the purchasing decision.
- **Interactive experiences:** Brands can create interactive campaigns that engage consumers in new and exciting ways.

Virtual Reality (VR)

- **Virtual tours:** VR offers immersive tours of locations or product experiences, allowing consumers to experience the brand in a unique way.
- **Virtual events:** Brands can organize virtual events that provide engaging and memorable experiences for attendees.

Application examples

- **IKEA Place:** An AR app that allows users to view IKEA furniture in their homes before making a purchase.
- **TOMS Virtual Giving Trip:** A VR experience that transports users on a giving trip, showcasing the impact of TOMS purchases on underserved communities.

Sustainability and purpose

Sustainability and social purpose are becoming increasingly important to consumers. Brands that adopt sustainable practices and demonstrate a genuine commitment to social causes are more likely to earn customer loyalty.

Sustainability strategies

- **Transparency:** Openly share your sustainable practices and your brand's positive impact on the environment and society.
- **Circular economy:** Adopt practices that promote reuse, recycling and waste reduction, creating a more sustainable product life cycle.

Application examples

- **Patagonia:** Known for its commitment to environmental sustainability, Patagonia promotes the repair and reuse of its products.
- **The Body Shop:** The company has a strong focus on fair trade, sustainability and ethical practices throughout its supply chain.

Digital branding and social influence

The role of social media and influencers is growing, and digital branding is becoming essential for reaching and engaging consumers.

Social media strategies

- **Authentic content:** Create authentic, engaging content that resonates with your target audience and drives engagement.
- **Influencer Partnerships:** Collaborate with influencers who share your brand values and have a relevant audience.

Application examples

- **Glossier:** The beauty brand uses social media to connect directly with consumers, encouraging user-

- generated content and creating a loyal community.
- **Red Bull:** The company creates high-impact content and collaborates with influencers and athletes to promote its brand in an authentic and engaging way.

Voice technology integration

Virtual assistants and voice devices like Amazon Alexa and Google Assistant are transforming the way consumers interact with brands.

Opportunities for Branding

- **SEO for voice:** Optimize your content for voice searches, ensuring your brand is easily found through virtual assistants.
- **Voice Experiences:** Create skills and apps for voice devices that deliver value to consumers and strengthen brand connection.

Application examples

- **Domino's Pizza:** Developed a skill for Alexa that allows customers to order pizza using voice commands.
- **Nestlé:** Created a recipe skill for Alexa, helping consumers find and prepare recipes using the brand's products.

ADAPTATION TO FUTURE TRENDS

Trend monitoring and analysis

Staying up to date with emerging trends is essential to adapting your branding strategies effectively.

Monitoring Tools

- **Google Trends:** Analyze search trends to identify changes in consumer behavior and preferences.
- **Hootsuite Insights:** Monitor social media

conversations to identify new trends and engagement opportunities.

Continuous innovation

Continuous innovation is crucial to keeping your brand relevant and competitive in an ever-changing market.

Innovation strategies

- **Research and development:** Invest in research and development to create innovative products and services that meet emerging consumer needs.
- **Customer feedback:** Use customer feedback to identify opportunities for improvement and innovation in your products and services.

Flexibility and adaptability

The ability to quickly adapt to changes in the market is a significant competitive advantage.

Adaptability strategies

- **Agile planning:** Adopt agile methodologies in your branding strategies to quickly respond to market changes and opportunities.
- **Testing and iteration:** Continuously test your campaigns and branding initiatives, iterating based on results to optimize effectiveness.

Future trends in branding offer exciting opportunities to innovate and connect with consumers in new and impactful ways. By anticipating and adopting these trends, you can strengthen your brand identity and ensure its long-term success.

In the next chapter, we'll explore specific strategies for small businesses and startups to develop strong brand identities, even with limited resources.

STRATEGIES FOR SMALL BUSINESSES AND STARTUPS

Developing a strong brand identity is crucial to the success of small businesses and startups, especially in competitive markets. In this chapter, we'll explore specific strategies that can help smaller businesses build and strengthen their brands, even with limited resources.

THE IMPORTANCE OF BRANDING FOR SMALL BUSINESS AND STARTUPS

For small businesses and startups, a strong brand can be the difference between success and failure. Effective branding helps differentiate the company in the market, build trust with customers and create a loyal consumer base.

BRANDING FUNDAMENTALS FOR SMALL BUSINESSES

Clear definition of the value proposition

A clear and unique value proposition is essential for attracting and retaining customers. It should communicate the unique benefits your company offers and why customers should choose you over competitors.

Steps to define the value proposition

- **Identify your differentiators:** Determine what makes your products or services unique.
- **Understand your target audience:** Know your audience's needs and wants.
- **Communicate clearly:** Create a clear, concise message that highlights the benefits of your offering.

Examples

- **Warby Parker:** "High-quality eyewear at affordable prices with the convenience of online shopping."
- **Dropbox:** "Simple, secure storage for all your files, accessible from anywhere."

Developing a cohesive visual identity

A strong and cohesive visual identity helps create recognition and credibility for your brand.

Visual identity elements

- **Logo:** Create a simple, memorable and versatile logo.
- **Color palette:** Choose colors that reflect the brand's personality and values.
- **Typography:** Select fonts that are legible and consistent with the brand tone.
- **Imagery:** Use images and graphics that resonate with the target audience and reinforce the brand's identity.

Examples

- **Mailchimp:** Utilizes a friendly logo and vibrant color palette that reflect its approachable and fun approach to email marketing.
- **Innocent Drinks:** Uses simple illustrations and soft colors to communicate an image of naturalness and health.

Brand Consistency

Maintaining consistency across all communications and touchpoints is essential to building a trustworthy and recognizable brand.

Steps to ensure consistency

- **Branding Guidelines:** Create a style guide that includes guidelines for logo usage, colors, typography, and tone of voice.
- **Staff training:** Ensure all employees understand and apply brand guidelines.
- **Regular review:** Regularly review all marketing materials and communications to ensure consistency.

Examples

- **Slack:** Maintains a consistent brand identity across platforms, with a vibrant color palette and a friendly, approachable tone of voice.
- **Glossier:** Uses soft colors and a minimalist style in all its communications, reinforcing its image as an accessible and modern beauty brand.

BRANDING STRATEGIES WITH LIMITED RESOURCES

Effective use of social media

Social media is a powerful and accessible tool for building and promoting your brand.

Social media strategies

- **Choosing the right platforms:** Focus on the platforms where your target audience is most active.
- **Authentic content:** Create authentic, engaging content that resonates with your audience.
- **Active engagement:** Interact with your followers by responding to comments and messages and participating in relevant conversations.

Examples

- **Away:** The luggage brand uses Instagram to share travel stories and inspiration, creating an engaged community around the brand.
- **Dollar Shave Club:** Uses humorous videos on social media to highlight its products and attract a young, relaxed audience.

Strategic partnerships

Forming partnerships with other companies can increase your brand's visibility and reach new audiences.

Types of partnerships

- **Co-branding:** Collaborate with complementary brands to create joint products or campaigns.
- **Local partnerships:** Work with local businesses for events, cross-promotions or community initiatives.
- **Influencers:** Collaborate with influencers who share your brand values and have a relevant audience.

Examples

- **GoPro and Red Bull:** Partnership that combined the emotion and adrenaline of the two brands in joint marketing campaigns.
- **Airbnb and Vice:** Created a series of experiences and content that highlight exclusive and authentic locations, attracting a young and adventurous audience.

Focus on customer service

Excellent customer service can turn customers into brand advocates, promoting word of mouth and loyalty.

Customer service strategies

- **Personalization:** Treat each customer as unique, personalizing interactions and solutions.
- **Speed and efficiency:** Respond quickly to queries and resolve issues efficiently.
- **Feedback:** Collect and use customer feedback to continually improve your products and services.

Examples

- **Zappos:** Known for its exceptional customer service, including offering free shipping and a streamlined returns process.
- **Chewy:** Famous for sending customers birthday

cards and flowers, creating an emotional connection and an extremely loyal customer base.

MEASURING THE SUCCESS OF BRANDING STRATEGIES

Performance indicators

Set key performance indicators (KPIs) to monitor the effectiveness of your branding strategies.

Important KPIs

- **Brand awareness:** Use social media research and analytics to measure brand awareness.
- **Customer Engagement:** Track social media engagement metrics such as likes, shares, and comments.
- **Customer loyalty:** Monitor retention rates and NPS (Net Promoter Score) to assess customer loyalty.

Continuous Feedback and Adjustments

Collect customer feedback and regularly analyze performance data to adjust your strategies as needed.

Feedback Tools

- **Satisfaction surveys:** Send regular surveys to collect customer opinions about your products and services.
- **Review Analysis:** Monitor comments on social media, review sites, and forums to identify trends and areas for improvement.

Developing a strong brand identity is essential to the success of small businesses and startups. By focusing on value proposition, visual identity, consistency and effective branding strategies, even with limited resources, your company can build a recognized and trusted brand that resonates with consumers and stands out in the market.

In the next chapter, we'll explore how brand partnerships and co-branding can strengthen your brand identity and expand your company's reach.

BRAND PARTNERSHIPS AND CO-BRANDING

Strategic partnerships and co-branding are powerful branding tools that can expand your brand's reach, increase credibility and create new market opportunities. In this chapter, we'll explore how to identify, form, and manage effective brand partnerships that strengthen your brand identity and drive success.

THE IMPORTANCE OF BRAND PARTNERSHIPS AND CO-BRANDING

Brand partnerships and co-branding allow two or more companies to combine their strengths and resources to create additional value for consumers. These collaborations can increase visibility, attract new audiences and reinforce brand identity.

TYPES OF BRAND PARTNERSHIPS

Co-branding

Co-branding involves two or more brands collaborating to create a joint product or service that combines each brand's strengths.

Co-Branding Examples

- **Nike and Apple:** The Nike+ partnership combines Apple technology with Nike sports products, delivering a seamless experience for consumers.
- **GoPro and Red Bull:** Both brands have teamed up to create exciting content and events, leveraging both companies' high-energy, adventurous image.

Promotional partnerships

These partnerships involve the joint promotion of products or services, often through marketing campaigns and events.

Examples of promotional partnerships

- **Uber and Spotify:** Uber users can connect their Spotify accounts and listen to their own playlists while traveling, improving the customer experience.
- **Starbucks and Barnes & Noble:** The two brands have

teamed up to offer Starbucks coffee inside Barnes & Noble stores, attracting more customers and creating a more enjoyable shopping experience.

Distribution partnerships

Distribution partnerships occur when one brand uses another's distribution network to reach new markets or improve the availability of its products.

Examples of Distribution Partnerships

- **Apple and AT&T:** The initial partnership between Apple and AT&T to launch the iPhone allowed Apple to utilize AT&T's distribution network and customer base to quickly reach a large audience.
- **Nestlé and Starbucks:** Nestlé distributes Starbucks coffee products in supermarkets and retailers, expanding the reach of the Starbucks brand.

Content Partnerships

These partnerships involve the joint creation of content, such as articles, videos or events, that promote both brands and provide value to the target audience.

Examples of Content Partnerships

- **Netflix and Marvel:** The two companies collaborated to create TV series based on Marvel characters, increasing the visibility and fan base of both brands.
- **National Geographic and The North Face:** Collaborated on content projects that highlight adventures and expeditions, reinforcing both brands' values of exploration and sustainability.

IDENTIFYING STRATEGIC PARTNERSHIPS

Alignment of values and target audience

Choose partners whose values and target audience align with

your brand. This ensures the partnership resonates well with consumers of both brands.

Selection criteria

- **Shared values:** Make sure both brands share similar values and principles.
- **Common Audience:** Identify partners who serve a similar target audience to yours to maximize the impact of the partnership.

Complementarity of products and services

Seek partnerships with brands whose products or services complement yours, creating a more attractive and complete offer for consumers.

Examples of complementarity

- **Technology and Fashion:** Partnerships between technology and fashion brands can create innovative products that combine style and functionality, such as smart watches and clothing with integrated technology.
- **Food and Beverage:** Food and beverage brands can come together to create new product combinations that appeal to consumers, such as gourmet snacks and artisanal beverages.

DEVELOPMENT AND IMPLEMENTATION OF PARTNERSHIPS

Planning and goal setting

Develop a detailed plan that defines the goals of the partnership, each brand's responsibilities, and the resources needed.

Steps for planning

- **Establish clear objectives:** Define what each brand hopes to achieve with the partnership, such as

increased sales, market expansion or strengthening the brand.
- **Determine responsibilities:** Specify each partner's responsibilities, including product development, marketing, and distribution.
- **Align resources:** Ensure both brands have the resources needed to successfully execute the partnership.

Contracts and agreements

Formalize the partnership with contracts and agreements that detail the terms, conditions and expectations of both parties.

Contract elements

- **Rights and obligations:** Clearly define the rights and obligations of each partner.
- **Intellectual property:** Establish how intellectual property will be shared and protected.
- **Contingency plans:** Include contingency plans to deal with potential problems or changes during the partnership.

Communication and coordination

Maintain open and regular communication between partners to ensure everyone is aligned and informed about the progress of the partnership.

Communication strategies

- **Regular Meetings:** Schedule regular meetings to discuss progress, resolve issues, and adjust strategies as needed.
- **Collaboration tools:** Use online collaboration tools like Slack or Trello to facilitate communication and coordination between teams.

MEASURING THE SUCCESS OF PARTNERSHIPS

Defining success metrics

Establish clear metrics to measure the success of the partnership and evaluate its impact.

Metric Examples

- **Increased sales:** Monitor the impact of the partnership on both partners' sales.
- **Customer engagement:** Track engagement metrics like social media interactions and customer feedback.
- **Brand awareness:** Use research and media analytics to measure the partnership's impact on brand awareness.

Continuous analysis and adjustments

Regularly analyze the data collected and make adjustments as needed to improve the effectiveness of the partnership.

Steps for analysis

- **Data collection:** Collect data on sales, engagement and other relevant metrics.
- **Performance analysis:** Compare results against established objectives to assess the success of the partnership.
- **Strategic adjustments:** Make adjustments to marketing, communications, and operations strategies as needed to maximize the benefits of the partnership.

Brand partnerships and co-branding offer valuable opportunities to strengthen brand identity, expand reach and create additional value for consumers. By identifying strategic partners, developing detailed plans, and measuring partnership success, you can maximize the benefits of these collaborations and drive your brand's growth.

In the next chapter, we will conclude our journey with strategies to maintain brand relevance and adapt to ongoing market needs.

MAINTAINING BRAND RELEVANCE

Maintaining brand relevance is an ongoing challenge that requires constant adaptation to market changes, technological innovations and evolving consumer expectations. In this concluding chapter, we'll explore strategies to ensure your brand remains relevant and adapted to ongoing market needs.

THE IMPORTANCE OF BRAND RELEVANCE

A relevant brand is one that continues to resonate with consumers over time, maintaining its competitive position and attracting new customers. Relevance is essential to sustaining growth, building loyalty and strengthening a brand's position in the market.

STRATEGIES TO MAINTAIN BRAND RELEVANCE

Continuous market monitoring

Staying up to date with market trends and consumer behavior is crucial to adjusting your branding strategies effectively.

Monitoring Tools

- **Google Trends:** Analyze search trends to identify changes in consumer preferences.
- **Hootsuite and Sprout Social:** Monitor conversations and trends on social media to capture market and consumer insights.

Continuous innovation

Constantly innovating products, services and marketing strategies helps keep the brand relevant and competitive.

Areas of innovation

- **Product development:** Invest in research and development to create products that meet emerging consumer needs.
- **Digital marketing:** Utilize new technologies and platforms to effectively reach and engage consumers.

- **Customer experience:** Continuously improve the customer experience to strengthen loyalty and satisfaction.

Examples

- **Tesla:** Continues to innovate in the automotive sector with electric vehicles and autonomous driving technologies.
- **Amazon:** Constantly invests in new technologies and services, such as drone delivery and the Alexa voice assistant, to improve customer convenience and experience.

Customer feedback and engagement

Collect and use customer feedback to adjust your strategies and ensure the brand meets consumers' expectations and needs.

Feedback Strategies

- **Satisfaction surveys:** Send regular surveys to collect customer opinions about your products and services.
- **Review Analysis:** Monitor comments on social media, review sites, and forums to identify trends and areas for improvement.
- **Engagement programs:** Create programs that encourage customer participation, such as loyalty clubs and online communities.

Examples

- **LEGO:** Utilizes the LEGO Ideas platform to enable fans to propose new product designs, engaging the community and innovating based on consumer feedback.
- **Starbucks:** Through the My Starbucks Idea program, the company collects customer suggestions and implements the best ideas, strengthening

engagement and loyalty.

Flexibility and adaptability

Being able to quickly adapt to market changes and new opportunities is a crucial competitive advantage.

Adaptability strategies

- **Agile planning:** Adopt agile methodologies in your branding strategies to quickly respond to market changes and opportunities.
- **Testing and iteration:** Continuously test your campaigns and branding initiatives, iterating based on results to optimize effectiveness.
- **Diversification:** Diversify your products and services to explore new markets and meet a broader range of consumer needs.

Examples

- **Netflix:** Evolved from a DVD rental service to a streaming giant, adapting to changes in consumer behavior and technology.
- **Adobe:** Transformed its business model from software licensing to a cloud-based subscription service, staying relevant in a rapidly evolving market.

MEASURING BRAND RELEVANCE

Performance indicators

Define and monitor key performance indicators (KPIs) to assess brand relevance over time.

Examples of KPIs

- **Brand awareness:** Use social media research and analytics to measure brand awareness.
- **Customer engagement:** Track engagement metrics

such as likes, shares, comments, and time spent on the site.
- **Customer satisfaction:** Monitor satisfaction rates and NPS (Net Promoter Score) to assess customer loyalty.
- **Market Growth:** Track market share and growth rates compared to competitors.

Continuous analysis and adjustments

Regularly analyze the data you collect and make adjustments as needed to ensure your brand remains relevant and competitive.

Steps for analysis

- **Data collection:** Collect data on sales, engagement and other relevant metrics.
- **Performance analysis:** Compare results with established objectives to evaluate the success of strategies.
- **Strategic adjustments:** Make adjustments to marketing, communications and operations strategies as needed to maximize brand relevance.

Maintaining brand relevance is an ongoing effort that requires constant vigilance, innovation and adaptation. By monitoring the market, continually innovating, engaging with customers and being flexible to changes, you can ensure your brand remains relevant and successful over the long term.

Congratulations on completing " **Brands That Sell: Effective Strategies for Creating and Strengthening Brand Identities** "! This book is designed to provide a comprehensive guide to developing and managing a strong, lasting brand identity. By applying the strategies and insights discussed, you will be well prepared to face branding challenges and achieve success in the competitive market.

As we turn the final page of this journey together, I sincerely hope that the learnings shared here have touched your heart and sparked new perspectives. If this book has brought you any value, I kindly ask that you take a few moments to leave a review on Amazon. Your words not only help me grow and hone my craft, but they also guide other readers in their quests for knowledge and inspiration. Your opinion is a valuable gift, both for me and for the community of readers looking for stories that transform. I sincerely thank you for sharing this journey with me and I hope we can meet again in the pages of a new adventure.

REGINALDO OSNILDO

Hello, I'm Reginaldo Osnildo, author and innovator in the areas of sales, technology, and communication strategies. My experience ranges from the academic environment, as a professor and researcher at the University of Southern Santa Catarina, to practice as a strategist at Grupo Catarinense de Rádios. With a PhD in sales narratives and digital convergence, and a master's degree in storytelling and social imaginary, I bring my readers a unique fusion of theory and practice. My goal is to provide knowledge in a simple, practical and didactic language, encouraging direct application in personal and professional life.

Yours sincerely

Reginaldo Osnildo

+55 48 991913865

reginaldoosnildo@gmail.com

www.ingramcontent.com/pod-product-compliance
Lightning Source LLC
Chambersburg PA
CBHW072050230526
45479CB00010B/646